DISCOVERING **DINOS**AURS

DINOSAUR
GIANTS

Jinny Johnson

Smart Apple Media

Published by Smart Apple Media,
an imprint of Black Rabbit Books
P.O. Box 3263, Mankato, Minnesota, 56002
www.blackrabbitbooks.com

Printed in the United States of America,
at Corporate Graphics in North Mankato, Minnesota.

Illustrated by Graham Rosewarne
Designed by Hel James
Edited by Mary-Jane Wilkins

Library of Congress Cataloging-in-Publication Data

Johnson, Jinny, 1949-
 Dinosaur giants / Jinny Johnson.
    p. cm. -- (Discovering dinosaurs)
 Audience: Grade 4 to 6.
 Summary: "Gives scientific facts about a number of
large species of dinosaurs"-- Provided by publisher.
 Includes index.
 ISBN 978-1-62588-013-0 (library binding)
1. Saurischia--Juvenile literature. 2. Dinosaurs--Juvenile
literature. [1. Dinosaurs.] I. Title.
 QE862.S3J637 2014
 567.913--dc23
                              2013003429

Picture credit
Front cover Merlinul/Shutterstock

DAD0511
052013
9 8 7 6 5 4 3 2 1

Contents

Inside a Dinosaur

A dinosaur was a kind of reptile that lived millions of years ago. We know about dinosaurs because many of their bones and teeth have been found.

Scientists divide the time when dinosaurs lived on Earth into three periods. These are called the Triassic, Jurassic, and Cretaceous. At the beginning of the Triassic period all the world's land was joined together. The land gradually split up into smaller areas to make the world we know today.

Triassic Period: 250–200 million years ago
Jurassic Period: 200–145 million years ago
Cretaceous Period: 145–65 million years ago

There weren't any people on Earth when dinosaurs were alive. This picture gives you an idea of how big each dinosaur was compared to a seven-year-old child.

Biggest of all the dinosaurs were the sauropods, such as **Brachiosaurus**. These long-necked monsters were the largest land animals ever.

This is what a Brachiosaurus looked like inside.

Bones: very strong
to support
enormous body

Ribs: longer
than an adult
human

Feet: big and
fleshy with
five toes

Brachiosaurus

Can you believe that there was once an animal that weighed as much as *12 elephants*? This was **Brachiosaurus**, one of the largest, **heaviest** creatures that has ever lived.

A full-grown Brachiosaurus had a huge body and a long, heavy tail. Its front legs measured 13 feet (4 m), which is more than two **tall** people standing on top of one another.

Only its head
was small—
about the
same size as
a horse's head.

Try saying this dinosaur's name:
Brak-ee-oh-sore-us

DINO FACTS
UP TO 100 FEET (30 M) LONG
LIVED 155–140 MILLION YEARS AGO

Finding Food

Brachiosaurus was a herbivore, which means that it only ate plants. Its long front legs allowed it to reach green leaves from the tallest trees. It chopped up the leaves with spoon-shaped teeth.

Fossilized footprints show that these dinosaurs moved around in herds. They couldn't move very fast because they were so **big** and **heavy**.

This is how big a sauropod footprint looks next to a human footprint.

Young Brachiosaurs

A female Brachiosaurus, like most dinosaurs, laid eggs. She may have laid about 100, each one about the size of a volleyball, and left them to hatch by themselves.

Baby brachiosaurs were tiny compared to their huge parents. They made a tasty meal for meat-eating dinosaurs, so they had to watch out for predators.

DINO FACTS
SAUROPODS LIKE
BRACHIOSAURUS MAY HAVE
LIVED TO BE 100 OR MORE.

Diplodocus

This monster had a long neck and an amazingly l o n g tail. It was one of the longest animals that has ever lived.

Diplodocus **was much lighter than Brachiosaurus because its bones were partly** hollow.

Try saying this dinosaur's name:
Dip-plod-oh-kus

Diplodocus had a small head and rows of teeth like little pegs. These were just the right size and shape for stripping leaves off plants.

This dinosaur could not chew its food, but may have swallowed stones to help grind the food down in its stomach.

Camarasaurus

Camarasaurus lived at about the same time as Diplodocus. It had **bigger teeth** so it could feed on **tougher** plants. This meant that the dinosaurs did not eat the same food.

Camarasaurus lived in herds, like most sauropods. The young dinosaurs probably stayed close to their parents for protection from predators.

Try saying this dinosaur's name: Kam-ar-a-sore-us

Apatosaurus

This **giant** sauropod was not quite as long as Diplodocus, but it was much heavier. It may have weighed 38 tons (34 tonnes). That's nearly as much as six elephants.

DINO FACTS
UP TO 70 FEET LONG (21 M)
LIVED 154–145 MILLION YEARS AGO

Hungry tyrannosaurs
sometimes tried
to attack these
huge dinosaurs.
A sauropod's only
weapon was its
long tail.

**Try saying this
dinosaur's name:
Ah-pat-oh-sore-us**

If a predator came too close,
Apatosaurus would lash out with its
tail and could even break an attacker's legs.

Mamenchisaurus

This sauropod had one of the longest necks of any animals ever. The neck had 19 e x t r a - l o n g bones and made up half of the dinosaur's length.

Mamenchisaurus was too big to move around in thick forest. But it could reach in with its long neck and feed on leaves from the trees.

Seismosaurus

The name of this dinosaur means **earth-shaking** lizard. It may have been the longest animal ever and measured 120–140 feet (36–42 m) from its nose to the tip of its whiplike tail. That's longer than six pickup trucks parked in a line.

Try saying this dinosaur's name:
Size-moh-sore-us

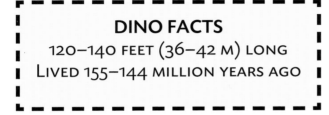

Seismosaurus didn't have to move very far as it could reach food all around with its l o n g n e c k.

Amargasaurus

This small sauropod had two rows of spines along its back. These may have helped to protect it from attackers. Or the spines may have been covered with skin and made the dinosaur look larger to warn off predators.

Amargasaurus could probably rear up on two legs to reach food or to scare off an enemy.

Try saying this dinosaur's name:
Ah-marg-ah-sore-us

DINO FACTS
Up to 39 feet
(12 m) long
Lived 132–127
million years ago

Words to Remember

fossils
Parts of an animal, such as bones and teeth, that have been preserved in rock over millions of years.

herd
A group of animals that move and feed together.

predator
An animal that hunts and kills other animals.

reptile
An animal with a backbone and a scaly body. Dinosaurs were reptiles. Today's reptiles include lizards, snakes, and crocodiles.

tyrannosaur
A type of large meat-eating dinosaur, such as Tyrannosaurus, which attacked plant-eating dinosaurs.

Index